Published in 2011 by Oberon Books Ltd
521 Caledonian Road, London N7 9RH
Tel: +44 (0) 20 7607 3637 / Fax: +44 (0) 20 7607 3629
info@oberonbooks.com
www.oberonbooks.com

Cover & book design: James Illman
Editor: Andrew Walby

Printed in Great Britain by CPI Antony Rowe, Chippenham.

ISBN: 978-1-84943-050-0

Front/back/inside front cover: Panayiotis Sinnos
Inside back cover: Hugo Glendinning

Right: William Trevitt (L) and Michael Nunn (R)

BALLET BOYZ

Michael Nunn & William Trevitt

"A couple of daring, funny blokes with a flair for the avant-garde"
The New York Times

OBERON BOOKS

LONDON

WWW.OBERONBOOKS.COM

PROL OGUE

The two of us met way back in 1985, while studying under Alexander Agadzhanov at The Royal Ballet School. Graduating into The Royal Ballet, we danced our way through the ranks, often understudying one another or paired together: Romeo and Mercutio, Des Grieux and Lescaut or as Zebra and Monkey. Alongside our performances in the classics, the highlight of each season would be in the making of new works with great choreographers like Sir Kenneth MacMillan, Glen Tetley, Twyla Tharp or William Forsythe. These experiences gave us the appetite for creation and creation has come to define us.

Our friendship developed through a shared passion for photography while still at The Royal Ballet. Pooling our money, we bought a camera and started clicking through rehearsals. The Royal Ballet encourages in-house talent and before long our pictures were being used for publicising the company, with credits under our pseudonym, George Piper (a combination of our middle names).

Our move into film and television started in 1997 with the announcement that the Royal Opera House would be closed for a complete rebuild. Goodbye to a structure imbued with historic, cultural glory. Whilst no one could deny the advantages of an efficient, modern replacement, there was real sadness at what would be lost so, more from a sense of duty than anything else, we decided to roll up our sleeves and record what the place meant to us.

Through the labyrinth of corridors, studios and dressing rooms we wanted to preserve our connection to a remarkable legacy. Armed with a video camera, we started filming and then, totally unexpectedly, found ourselves in the eye of a major political and cultural storm.

Left: Michael with Viviana Durante in Sir Kenneth MacMillan's *Requiem*
Above: Billy with Darcey Bussell in Glen Tetley's *La Ronde*

Below: An example of some of our early photographic experimentation and the beginning of our friendship with Hugo Glendinning, whom we met when we were both featured as 'up-and-coming artists' in *Time Out* magazine (2nd January 1991)

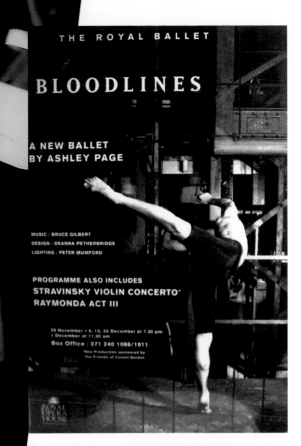

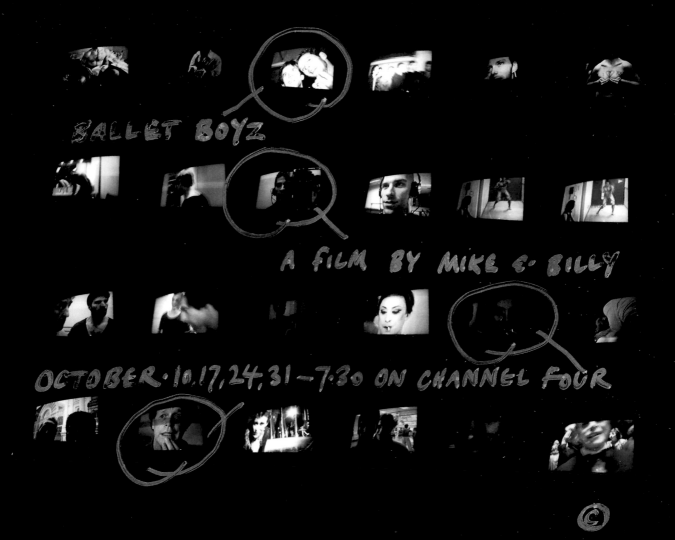

BALLET BOYZ

A FILM BY MIKE & BILLY

OCTOBER · 10,17,24,31 — 7·30 ON CHANNEL FOUR

The Royal Opera House was under fire in Parliament, where questions were being asked of its management and governance. Even the future of The Royal Ballet was in jeopardy but throughout this chaos we kept our camera rolling.

Feeling that it would make an interesting documentary we showed the footage of these turbulent events to television producer and former Royal Ballet dancer Ross MacGibbon. He pitched it to Channel 4 who took the risk and broadcast our first television series: *Ballet Boyz*. Ross had coined the name and we hated it. However, titles have never been our strong suit and, unable to come up with an alternative, we became

By the time *Ballet Boyz* aired we had decided to leave The Royal Ballet and in 1999, with fellow Royal Ballet dancers Stuart Cassidy, Gary Avis, Matthew Dibble and Tetsuya Kumakawa, we set out to form our own company, K Ballet, in Japan. We toured the country for two years and were enormously popular with Japanese audiences. This formative period featured in our second documentary series for Channel 4, *Ballet Boyz II: The Next Step*.

Our ambition was to explore different dance styles and commission new work. However, the reality was less than challenging and, disillusioned with the same old crowd pleasers, we decided to return to England

POINT
LESS

FIRST PERFORMANCE: THE ROUNDHOUSE
15TH OCTOBER 2001

REPERTOIRE: *STEPTEXT* (WILLIAM FORSYTHE)
SIGUE (PAUL LIGHTFOOT & SOL LEÓN)
TANGOID (NUNN & TREVITT)
MOMENTS OF PLASTIC JUBILATION (NUNN & TREVITT)
CRITICAL MASS (RUSSELL MALIPHANT)

CAST: MICHAEL NUNN, WILLIAM TREVITT,
OXANA PANCHENKO, MATTHEW HART, CHRIS MARNEY,
JUSTINE DOSWELL, LUCY DODD

AWARDS: NOMINATED FOR THE SOUTH BANK SHOW AWARDS

OXANA PANCHENKO, WINNER OF THE TIME OUT AWARD
FOR OUTSTANDING PERFORMANCE IN *STEPTEXT*

George Piper had been our alter ego as photographers. Now it was time for him to dance. Our first show as George Piper Dances, entitled *Pointless*, was performed in London at the legendary Roundhouse. This was before its renovation and it was up to us to bring everything in; the stage, the seats, the lights – even the toilets!

A generous benefactor gave us the start-up money to cover our first year of operations but a desire to make an impact on the scene urged us to spend the entire amount on one week of performances. It was all new – a huge risk – but also incredibly exciting; we felt like pioneers, creating something unique. It is still one of our proudest achievements.

Dear Audience

George Piper Dances is the result of many years of collaboration between us, culminating in this, our first season of performances.

Our aim is to present theatre of the highest quality, bringing together a collection of World renowned choreographers, composers and artists.

We will present work that not only challenges, but also entertains. By doing this we believe our audience will broaden and grow as we do, extending our horizons in every direction.

Enjoy the evening
love
Michael & Billy.

Above: Our manifesto! An open letter to our first audience printed in the programme

Lack of money made it impossible to bring the big-name choreographers to us so we went to them. To Nederlands Dans Theater in Holland to work with Paul Lightfoot and Sol León and to Germany where William Forsythe kindly fitted our rehearsals around his Ballett Frankfurt schedule, working with us in his lunch breaks and after hours.

Also, we coveted *Critical Mass*, a duet by Russell Maliphant and approached him for the permission to dance it. Unfortunately, he said no. Never ones to give up, we got hold of a recording and learnt it move by move before persuading Russell to take a look at what we'd done. This time he said yes. We like to think that he admired our balls.

Next page: *Moments of Plastic Jubilation*

GEORGE PIPER DANCES PRESENT CHANNEL 4 'BALLET BOYZ'

MICHAEL NUNN & WILLIAM TREVITT

pointless

'Britain's most off-the-wall ballet dancers'

DAILY TELEGRAPH

Photo: George Piper

october 15 | 16 | 17 | 18 | 19 | 20

roundhouse
The Roundhouse Chalk Farm Road London NW1

Evening Standard
arena
JERWOOD SPACE

Ticketselect 020 7494 5386
www.gpdances.com

gpd

Above: Southwark, South London. A boxing ring seemed appropriate for this poster shoot, in order to match the intensity of Russell Maliphant's choreography, *Critical Mass*.

Tango

- pull away to M lies down.
- rgt. sideways knee on thigh dodge.
- bit we know
- shoulder sit swing swing swing
  1 kneel swing — run —
- we know (bird jump)
- M solo
- jete ... port des bras
- 3 aides
- jump off my back (headstand)
- run 23 to corner
- Envelopé jump (2nd) run to corner
- bendy knees → sit arm over
- pop lie down 1st funny jump / M up / Bup

2 hitches in line   barrel / pirouette →
bof lift
Polka pirouette   waft facing back

3 swings into [M kick lift] !

1st thru unison thrust = Munn
2 slow = synched — shunp (bump M push arm)
3 slowish — Munn fall on jst before end.
4 triple — 16 inches — fumble it in gym
Legs = crazy arms. Canoe.
Wait = dynamic hur.
2 x 8 of small cymbals
big cymbal: double fuck

3rd
- Buck
- knee
- slow
- Usua

Surprise
- Pivot
  up side

crawl a
- lift lift
  scuff c

Ran Dos

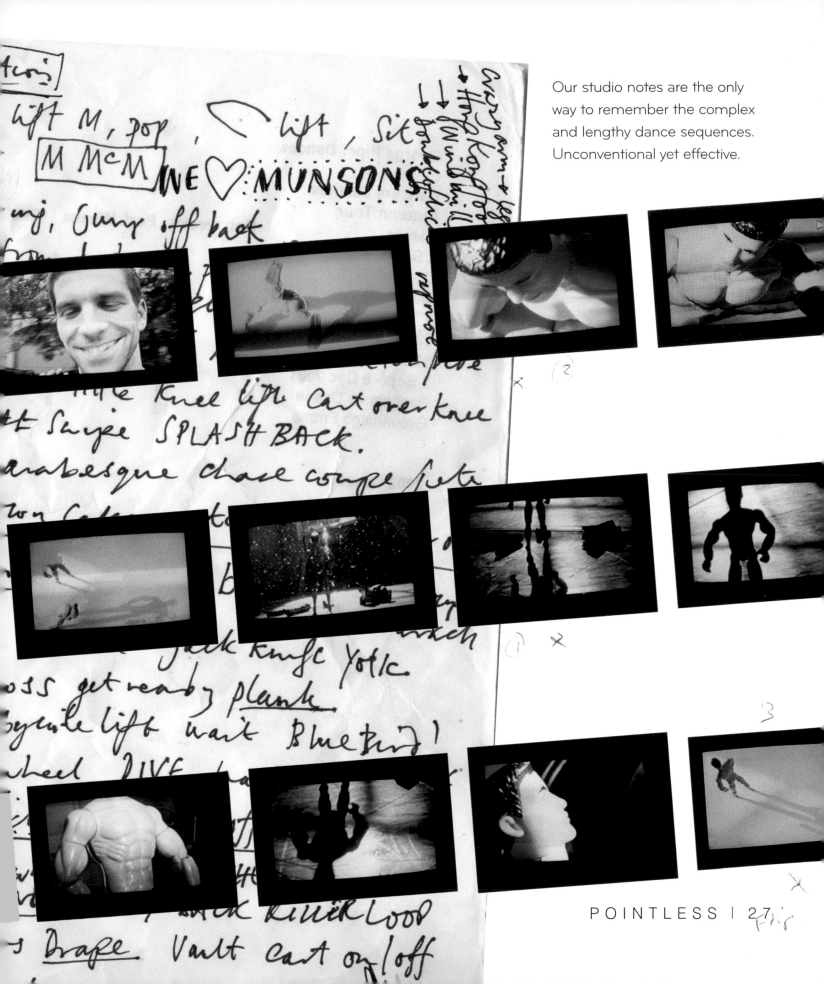

Our studio notes are the only way to remember the complex and lengthy dance sequences. Unconventional yet effective.

Above: *Critical Mass*

Above: With Oxana in *Steptext*

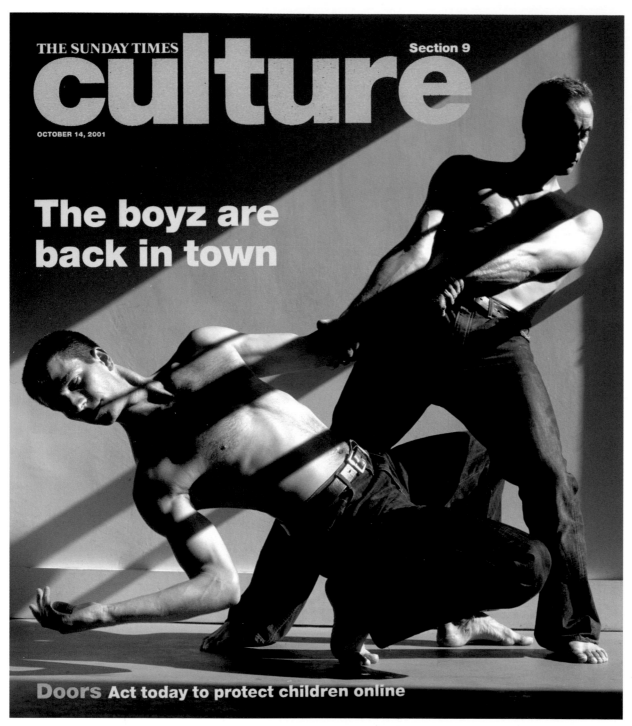

Above: Our first *Sunday Times Culture* magazine cover, taken by
Hugo Glendinning in a five minute break in rehearsals (14th October 2001)

Above: With Billy's sons, Zachary and Joseph, taken for the inside of our programme to promote dance in education, especially for boys

Having used film in our live shows, documentary making had become a serious pursuit. We were also interested in dance for camera and an opportunity to explore this arose in 2003 when we were asked to curate and present the Channel 4 series *4Dance*.

Stealth was shot in France by fashion photographer Julian Broad and featured the very young Joseph and Zachary Trevitt as our body doubles.

Suit of Light was directed by Margaret Williams and was inspired by the father of classical ballet Louis XIV – The Sun King. The costume was created by wedding dress designer Neil Cunningham from hi-vis fabric that appeared to emit light.

Torsion Unwound was choreographed by Russell Maliphant and shot by our old friend Hugo Glendinning in his home studio. The 'rain' effect was courtesy of Hugo's shower hose.

CRITICS' CHOICE

★★★★★

FIRST PERFORMANCE: QUEEN ELIZABETH HALL
25TH MARCH, 2003

REPERTOIRE: *RED OR WHITE* (AKRAM KHAN)
MESMERICS (CHRISTOPHER WHEELDON)
SATIE STUD. (MICHAEL CLARK)
TRIO (RUSSELL MALIPHANT)
DEAREST LOVE (MATTHEW BOURNE)

CAST: MICHAEL NUNN, WILLIAM TREVITT, OXANA PANCHENKO,
MATTHEW HART, HUBERT ESSAKOW

AWARDS: WINNER OF THE 2003 THEATRICAL MANAGEMENT
ASSOCIATION AWARD FOR OUTSTANDING ACHIEVEMENT IN
DANCE

OXANA PANCHENKO, WINNER OF THE CRITICS' CIRCLE
NATIONAL DANCE AWARD FOR OUTSTANDING FEMALE ARTIST

Red or White
Choreographer:
Akram Khan

Satie Stud.
Choreographer:
Michael Clark

Dearest Love
Choreographer:
Matthew Bourne

Mesmerics
Choreographer:
Christopher Wheeldon

Trio
Choreographer:
Russell Maliphant

We had become fascinated by the ways in which different choreographers work and began to develop an idea for a show in which we would give five critically acclaimed choreographers two weeks each to create work for us. We filmed the process, documenting their different approaches and methods. Each film was shown as an introduction to the piece before it was seen on stage.

Critics' Choice ★ ★ ★ ★ ★ has to be the best title we have come up with so far. Not only were we using five star choreographers but all press reviews would have to start with '*Critics' Choice* ★ ★ ★ ★ ★', which is the holy grail for any review. Channel 4 liked it so much they commissioned a television show based on the concept: *The Rough Guide to Choreography*.

Top: With Beadie Finzi
Bottom: Monica Zamora

We made *The Rough Guide to Choreography* with filmmaker Beadie Finzi. The programme posed the question: Are true choreographers born or made?

Having worked with many of the greats we were keen to discover whether any of their genius had rubbed off on us. The programme culminated in a live show at the Barbican where we presented our own choreography, *Follow*, and in doing so answered the question.

Top: Oxana
Left: With Beadie Finzi

Left: Michael with Monica in *Follow*
Above: Oxana and Hubert

Abstract choreography is the norm in contemporary dance. It had been a while since we'd gone on stage as characters and we were beginning to miss it so we created *Naked*, a hybrid of contemporary movement with characters and storylines. Hugo Glendinning joined us in developing an evocative video environment that would be projected on to Bob Crowley's brilliant set design.

It was a huge production. The stress nearly killed us.

Above: Hugo

Above: The cast of *Naked* relax on set before the show

Above: With Bob in his studio checking out the set design

Above: Billy with Monica in *Naked*

Left: Projection tests on Billy
Above: With Monica in a publicity still

NAKED | 53

RISE & FALL

FIRST PERFORMANCE OF *BROKEN FALL*:
THE ROYAL OPERA HOUSE, 3RD DECEMBER, 2003

CHOREOGRAPHY: RUSSELL MALIPHANT

REPERTOIRE: *TORSION* (MUSIC: RICHARD ENGLISH)
TWO (MUSIC: ANDY COWTON)
BROKEN FALL (MUSIC: BARRY ADAMSON)

We had worked with Sylvie Guillem whilst at The Royal Ballet, sometimes in the classics as her suitors in *The Sleeping Beauty*, sometimes in modern choreography like William Forsythe's *Steptext*. In 2002 we invited Sylvie to The Place Theatre to watch the first show of *Torsion*, a 25-minute duet created for us by Russell Maliphant. Long story short: she came, she saw, she liked and Russell made a trio for us, *Broken Fall*. Because of conflicts in our schedules it took almost a year to complete, but finally *Broken Fall* had its World Premiere at the Royal Opera House and after a five-year absence we returned, triumphant, to The Royal Ballet as Principal Guest Artists.

Above and right: Publicity shots for *Broken Fall*

Right: With Oxana in *Broken Fall*

Broken Fall was a massive success and we went on to combine it with other works by Russell: *Two*, a solo for Sylvie, and our duet *Torsion*, in a show called *Rise and Fall* which toured the world for the next two years.

Broken Fall won Best New Dance Production at the Oliviers in 2004.

Top left: Michael on Shibuya Crossing, Tokyo – the largest pedestrian crossing in the world
Bottom left: Mr and Mrs Nunn and Mr and Mrs Trevitt in Paris to see their Boyz

Opposite page
Top right: In Japan
Middle right: With Satoko Ishikawa
Bottom right: Waiting to rehearse

Following the success of *Rise and Fall* on the stage, we pitched the idea of filming the works as individual pieces. This was the first commission from Channel 4 for our newly formed television production company, Ballet Boyz Productions. For each film we selected a different director. *Broken Fall* was realised by BAFTA award winner David Hinton, *Two* by music video director Dominic Leung and *Torsion* by maverick filmmaker Grant Gee.

The project was something of a watershed for us and felt like a massive step forward, particularly on the first day of shooting, seeing a crew of fifty at Pinewood Studios, all there to capture us and Sylvie skipping around to music!

Top left: With Russell filming *Torsion*

Filming *Torsion* at The Old Truman Brewery, East London

With Sylvie Guillem filming *Broken Fall* at Pinewood Studios

ENCORE

FIRST PERFORMANCE: SADLER'S WELLS
26TH SEPTEMBER, 2006

REPERTOIRE:

MANDOX BANDOX
CHOREOGRAPHY: RAFAEL BONACHELA,
MUSIC: ANDY COWTON
ARRANGEMENT: BEN FOSKETT
LIGHTING DESIGN: NATASHA CHIVERS

JJANKE
CHOREOGRAPHY: CHARLES LINEHAN
MUSIC: BRATKO BIBIČ
LIGHTING DESIGN: MIKAEL SYLVEST

PROPELLER
CHOREOGRAPHY: LIV LORENT
MUSIC: VIVALDI, EZIO BOSSO
LIGHTING DESIGN: NATASHA CHIVERS
COSTUME DESIGN: PAUL SHRIEK

ON CLASSICISM
CHOREOGRAPHY: WILL TUCKETT
MUSIC: JS BACH
LIGHTING: NATASHA CHIVERS

CAST: MICHAEL NUNN, WILLIAM TREVITT, OXANA PANCHENKO

Above: Original poster artwork by Natasha Law

In 2006 we danced at the Sydney Festival, which meant spending January in Australia and hanging out with the other performers. One night we were able to catch the end of Elvis Costello's show and were struck by how cool it would be to do an encore. It's almost impossible with dance so we formed a band. We bought some instruments and, along with Oxana, we learnt how to play them. Exploring a vast repertoire we eventually settled on *I Bet That You Look Good On The Dance Floor* by the Arctic Monkeys, which we nailed as an encore for our new show *Encore*. Another highlight and a glimpse at an easier life.

For the film element of this show we asked our friend and journalist Charlie Stayt to give us a tough interview, forcing us to justify our art form. What started out as a fun concept ended as a profound reminder of why we've dedicated ourselves to the arts.

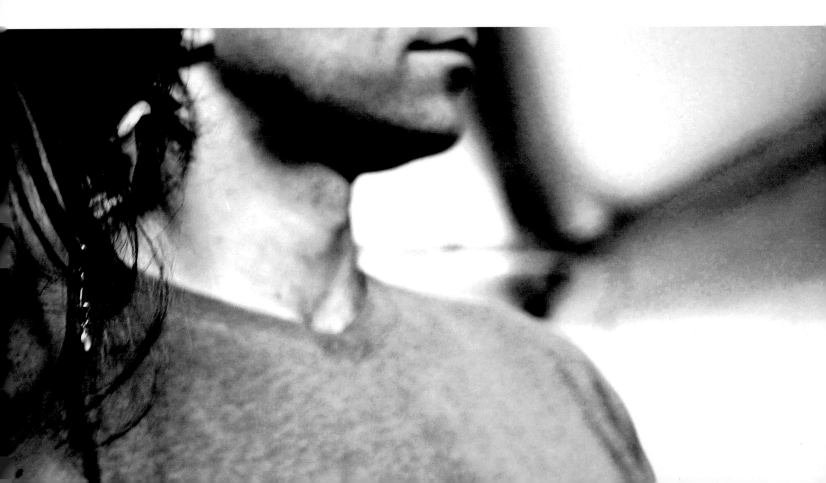

Above: *Jjanke*
Left: Michael with Oxana in *Propeller*

Above: The original line up: Oxana on bass, Billy on lead guitar and Michael on drums and vocals

WING BENDER
KNOB DROP
DOUBLE DOWN GEORGIAN
FLIP FLOP
CAT SWING CAT, SUPER SWING CAT
SUPER FAKE SWING CAT
RODEO
RACHEL VON MOOSE
POLISH

Above: Another example of Ballet Boyz studio notes for *Jjanke*

When Christopher Wheeldon told us he was going to Moscow and would be the first Englishman to make a ballet for the Bolshoi, 'The largest, most famous and probably most difficult-to-work-with ballet company in the world,' we knew we'd have to make a documentary about his experience.

We moved into a Moscow apartment for three months with filmmaker Oliver Manzi together with our colleague Oxana, who joined us as interpreter. Filming every day we watched on helplessly as Chris struggled to communicate his new ideas in the studio. He likes input from dancers when creating a work whereas the Russians simply wanted to be given their steps. Finally, the only solution was for us to put down our cameras and dance him out of trouble. We'd worked with Chris enough for him to be able to comfortably create on us and then transfer the choreography to the Russian dancers.

It was a terrifying, on-the-edge-of-disaster kind of experience, but ultimately rewarding. Even the film edit was exhausting, but at least we got to work with a composer we've admired for a long time, Ezio Bosso, who created an original score for the finished film.

In 2008 *Strictly Bolshoi* won the prestigious Rose d'Or for Best Arts Documentary, a tremendous honour and our first award for filmmaking. Then, later that year, we learned that we had been nominated for an International Emmy for Best Arts Film. We were in the States filming another project and so made a detour to the awards ceremony in New York.

Seated right at the back of the room, next to the kitchens, we assumed that we had no chance of winning. It was a long walk to the stage when our names were announced! As our commissioning editor at Channel 4, Jan Younghusband said: 'An Emmy! Wow! Not bad for a film made on a shoestring and cut on a laptop in your Islington toilet. Well done Boyz.'

BALLET FOR THE PEOPLE

FIRST PERFORMANCE: THE ROYAL FESTIVAL HALL
14TH JULY, 2007

SPECIAL COMMISSIONS: *AMOX* (RAFAEL BONACHELA),
ON BEFORE (WILL TUCKETT),
RIAPERTURA (BALLET BOYZ / CHRISTOPHER WHEELDON),
YUMBA VS. NONINO (CRAIG REVEL-HORWOOD)

REPERTOIRE: RAMBERT, ENGLISH NATIONAL BALLET,
BIRMINGHAM ROYAL BALLET, THE ROYAL BALLET – BELINDA
HATLEY IN ASHTON'S *FIVE BRAHMS WALTZES IN THE MANNER
OF ISADORA DUNCAN*

CAST: MICHAEL NUNN, WILLIAM TREVITT, OXANA PANCHENKO,
AMY HOLLINGSWORTH, ZENAIDA YANOWSKY,
CHRISTOPHER WHEELDON, BELINDA HATLEY

LIGHTING DESIGN: NATASHA CHIVERS

An honour has been bestowed upon us. That's how it felt to be asked to curate a Gala to celebrate the reopening of the wonderful Royal Festival Hall. We came up with a great idea: we offered money to The Royal Ballet, English National Ballet, Birmingham Royal Ballet and Rambert Dance Company to create new ballets for the Gala. Surprisingly, none of them took us up on the offer. So we used the cash to commission new works for ourselves.

We co-created *Riapertura* with Christopher Wheeldon and Ezio Bosso, in which Chris danced with Michael and Oxana. Will Tuckett made *On Before*, a duet for Billy and Royal Ballet Principal Zenaida Yanowsky. Rafael Bonachela made *Amox*, a duet for Oxana and Amy Hollingsworth and Craig Revel-Horwood created a tango for us, *Yumba vs. Nonino*, our most popular commission to date.

Yumba vs. Nonino

When Darcey announced her retirement from The Royal Ballet we offered to produce a farewell Gala for her at Sadler's Wells. For this she chose some of her all-time favourite pieces to perform and we staged the show, gathering a glittering cast of her Royal Ballet colleagues. During the performance we screened several intimate interviews in which she reflected on her time as a dancer and her forthcoming retirement.

The show was commended as a fitting and moving tribute to one of this country's finest dancers and was Sadler's Wells' fastest-selling show, ever!

It's Chris Wheeldon here calling from New York,

GREAT EST HITS

FIRST PERFORMANCE: SADLER'S WELLS
7TH MAY 2008

REPERTOIRE: *BROKEN FALL* (RUSSELL MALIPHANT),
MESMERICS (CHRISTOPHER WHEELDON),
EDOX (RAFAEL BONACHELA),
YUMBA VS. NONINO (CRAIG REVEL-HORWOOD)

CAST: MICHAEL NUNN, WILLIAM TREVITT,
OXANA PANCHENKO, TIM MORRIS, EDWARD WATSON,
MALGORZATA DZIERZON

LIGHTING: MICHAEL HULLS, NATASHA CHIVERS

Greatest Hits was a chance to put some of our favourite
pieces together in one show. As simple as that.

Yumba vs. Nonino

Edox with Oxana, Edward Watson and Ezio Bosso

EXODUS III

When our friend, fellow artist and equine conservationist Francesca Kelly invited us to make a film involving her beautiful and rare Marwari horses, we jumped at the chance. The Marwari are an ancient breed from the Jodhpur region of India with distinctive inward-turned ear tips.

The film was shot entirely on Chappaquiddick, Massachusetts in the winter of 2007. Although Billy had never been diving before, he managed to capture some spectacular images whilst being held on the bottom of the ocean, by friend, ex-Royal Ballet colleague and professional diver, Anthony Bourne. It was a crazy and wonderful week's work and we thank you, Francesca, for the opportunity.

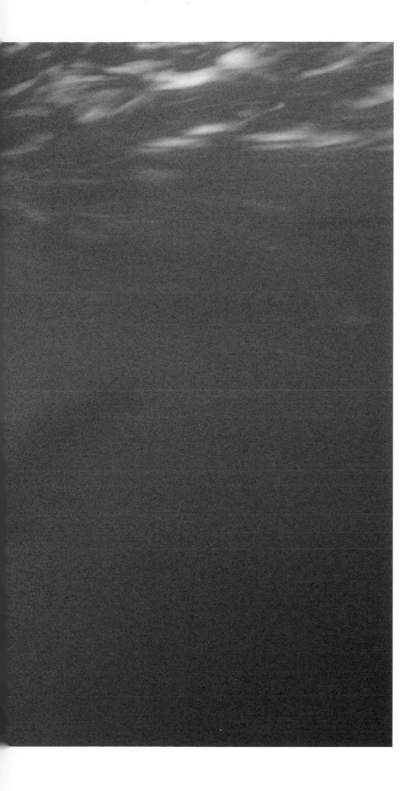

ELECTRIC COUNTER POINT

FIRST PERFORMANCE: THE ROYAL OPERA HOUSE
28TH FEBRUARY, 2008

CHOREOGRAPHY: CHRISTOPHER WHEELDON

MUSIC: JS BACH, STEVE REICH, MUKUL

LIGHTING DESIGN: NATASHA CHIVERS

COSTUME DESIGN: JEAN-MARC PUISSANT

VIDEOGRAPHY: MICHAEL NUNN & WILLIAM TREVITT

With Royal Ballet dancers Natalie Harrison and Kenta Kura

Whilst in Russia, usually under the influence of vodka, we talked with Christopher Wheeldon about how dance and film could mix. When he was commissioned to make a new, one-act work for The Royal Ballet it seemed like the perfect opportunity to put our ideas into practice. The Royal Opera House built a mock-up of the set in one of their gigantic rehearsal rooms and we kitted it out as a Blue Screen studio.

We filmed the four soloists so that we could reproduce them into a virtual *corps de ballet*. This created a technological nightmare but the finished effect was beautiful and totally arresting.

Left and above: Eric Underwood, Leanne Benjamin and Sarah Lamb
Next page: Marianela Nuñez

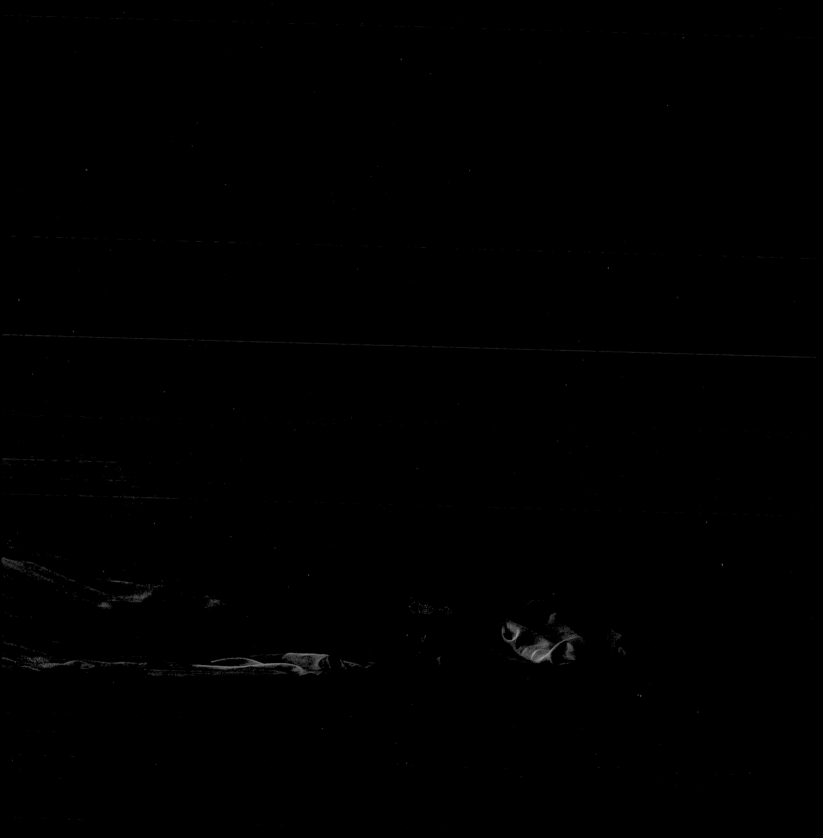

In the summer of 2009 The Royal Ballet became the first international ballet company to visit Cuba since Fidel Castro's revolution. We got ourselves a passage on that trip to make a documentary film about it.

Cuban-born Carlos Acosta starred in the shows: this was a chance for Carlos to show his countrymen who he'd been dancing with since his departure. We supplied two large projection screens and relayed the performances from the theatre to the main square in Havana where thousands of cheering Cubans witnessed this historic event, free of charge.

This is for you, this is for all of you!

Left: Carlos Acosta and Tamara Rojo in *Le Corsaire*
Above: In the main square after the show

MARGOT

DIRECTOR: OTTO BATHURST

PRODUCER: CELIA DUVAL FOR MAMMOTH SCREEN LTD.

WRITER: AMANDA COE

STAGE DIRECTION: MICHAEL NUNN & WILLIAM TREVITT

CAST: ANNE-MARIE DUFF, MICHIEL HUISMAN

TRANSMISSION DATE: BBC FOUR, 30TH NOVEMBER, 2009

When we were asked to help recreate the lives of Margot Fonteyn and Rudolf Nureyev for a BBC drama in 2009, we knew at once that this was a major challenge. Our job was to teach the actors, Anne-Marie Duff and Michiel Huisman, to carry themselves as dancers so that they might, with the right camera angles and dancing body doubles, convince us that they were the most famous ballet partnership in history.

BALLET BOYZ THE RITE OF SPRING

DIRECTORS: MICHAEL NUNN, WILLIAM TREVITT, GRANT GEE

PRODUCER: KERRY WHELAN FOR BALLET BOYZ PRODUCTIONS LTD

MUSIC: IGOR STRAVINSKY

CHOREOGRAPHY: PAUL ROBERTS, FREDDIE OPOKU-ADDAIE, KEVIN GOPIE

COSTUME DESIGN: SHELINA SOMANI

STAGING: MIKE LINDSAY, JAMES FICKLING, SWOOSHED

TRANSMISSION DATE: BBC THREE, 23RD DECEMBER, 2009

AWARDS: WINNER OF THE 2010 GOLDEN PRAGUE GRAND JURY PRIZE, NOMINATIONS FOR ROSE D'OR BEST ARTS DOCUMENTARY AND BEST SOCIAL FILM

Top left to right: Paul Roberts and Layla Ellison; Michael and Shelina Somani; Freddie Opoku-Addaie; Grant Gee; Kevin Gopie

In 2009 we were asked to reimagine *The Rite of Spring* for the BBC. Many different styles of dance would have to be involved, everything from break-dance to ballroom with a little bit of pole-dancing thrown into the mix. It was a big job to pull off with a very tight turnaround but was made possible by the commitment of the team around us. The film went on to win the Grand Jury Prize at the 2010 Golden Prague International Television Awards.

Above and right: In rehearsal

Above: Two of our Sirens, Sarah Robinson and Katie Collins

Above: Jean Sharman, our Tribal Queen

Above: The final moment. Leon Poulton as the Sacrificial Virgin
Right: Chantelle Pritchard, shot from our pole camera

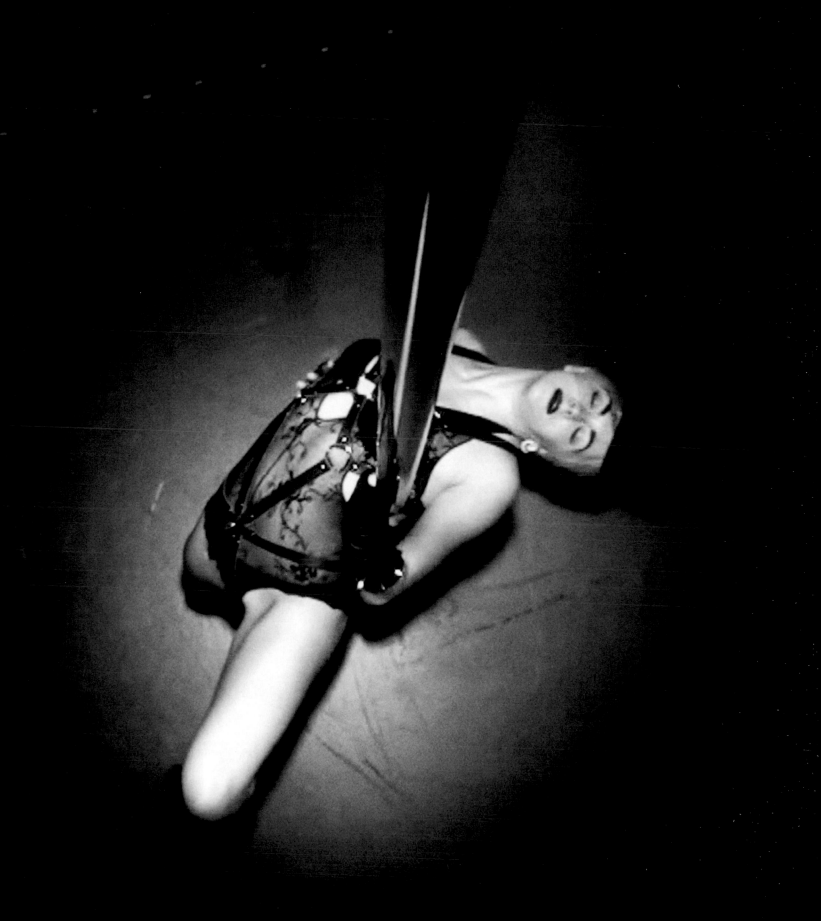

THE
TALENT

In 2009 we embarked on our latest adventure, a new all-male company of dancers known as *the* TALENT, the next generation of Ballet Boyz. Selected by open audition, we recruited young dancers, all with different dance backgrounds but with exceptional talent and the same spirit we like to think we had at their age.

Their first outing was in spring 2010 with new work *B_Banned* by Freddie Opoku-Addaie, *Alpha* by Paul Roberts and a reworking of our original duet *Torsion*, reset by Russell Maliphant for six dancers.

In summer 2010 we took the company to Martha's Vineyard in Massachusetts for two weeks of study and development, working with a range of teachers and choreographers including Carla Maxwell and David Dorfman.

In spring 2011 *the* TALENT completed their first Sadler's Wells season with a show comprising *Torsion*, *Alpha* and a new commission, *Void*, by Czech choreographer Jarek Cemerek.

Left: Paul Roberts' *Alpha*
Above: Russell Maliphant's *Torsion*

Above: *B_Banned*
Right: Matt Rees and Leon Poulton in *Torsion*

Above: *Void*
Next page: Jesús Sanz in *Void*

Training in Massachusetts:
Edward Pearce, Taylor Benjamin,
Miguel Esteves, Jesús Sanz

At the time of writing, *the* TALENT goes from strength to strength. We are really enjoying working with them and watching them develop as artists.

We ourselves haven't danced for a while but will always be dancers and may find ourselves on stage again before too long. We are also keen to make more films, both documentary and drama.

For this rich and fulfilling working life, we consider ourselves lucky.

A FEW OF THE PEOPLE WHO HELPED ALONG THE WAY

STAFF
Nina Baker
Sue Banner
Sarah Dekker
Fleur Derbyshire Fox
Anne Gallacher
Rebecca Hanson
Adam Lawford
Peter Leone
James McMenemy
Tim Morris
Fern Potter
Katherine Rothman
Louise Shand-Brown
Mark Slaughter
Rebecca Trevitt
Angela Whelan
Kerry Whelan

TRUSTEES
Philip Reed
Mary Anne Cordeiro
Vivien Duffield
Angus Forbes
Kate Gavron
Tom Hope
Gillian Karran-Cumberlege
Paul Postle
Louise Shand-Brown

DANCERS
Corey Baker
Taylor Benjamin
Joss Carter
Joe Darby
Zack Dennis
Lucy Dodd
Justine Doswell
Kai Downham
Viviana Durante
Iestyn Edwards
Hubert Essakow
Miguel Esteves
Sylvie Guillem
Yvette Halfhide
Matthew Hart
Belinda Hatley
Amy Hollingsworth
Davin King
Adam Kirkham
Thomas Linecar
Christopher Marney
Anthony Middleton
Leire Ortueta
Oxana Panchenko
Edward Pearce
Leon Poulton
Matt Rees
Jesús Sanz
Edward Watson
Christopher Wheeldon
Zenaida Yanowsky
Monica Zamora

CHOREOGRAPHERS
Mauro Bigonzetti
Rafael Bonachela
Matthew Bourne
Jarek Cemerek
Michael Clark
Layla Ellison
William Forsythe
Kevin Gopie
Matthew Hart
Amy Hollingsworth
Akram Khan
Sol Leon
Paul Lightfoot
Charles Linehan
Liv Lorent
Russell Maliphant
Cathy Marston
Freddie Opoku-Addaie
Craig Revel-Horwood
Paul Roberts
Will Tuckett
Christopher Wheeldon

COMPOSERS
Barry Adamson
X Alfonso
Ezio Bosso
Fernando Corona
Andy Cowton
Ondrej Dedecek
Richard English
Ben Foskett
Keaton Henson
Mukul
Murcof
Sarah Shanson
Julian Swales

DESIGNERS
Andrew Atkinson
Peter Avery
Jon Bausor
Simon Bennison
Hussein Chalayan
Natasha Chivers
Paule Constable
Ros Coombes
Bob Crowley
Neil Cunningham
Cathy de Monchaux
Fotini Dimou
Andrew Ellis
Zerlina Hughes
Michael Hulls
Julius Lumsden
Aideen Malone
Abraham Papacosta
Paul Shriek
Shelina Somani
Mikael Sylvest
Karsten Tinapp
Tony Wood

MUSICIANS
John Barwood
Bratko Bibic
Ezio Bosso
Mark Cox
Sonya Fairbairn
Ninon Foiret
Richard Friedman
Andrew Fuller
Philip Gammon
Robert Gibbs
Nigel Goodwin
Jonathan Higgins
Philippa Ibbotson
Julia Knight
Zoe Martlew
Fiona McNaught
Al Mobbs
Rus Pearson
Dave Price
Clive Williamson

FILM
Julian Broad
Claudia Calvino
Jerry Chater
Amanda Coe
Stuart Douglas
Beadie Finzi
Grant Gee
Hugo Glendinning
David Hinton
Tabitha Jackson
Matt Killip
Tariq Kubasi
Dominic Leung
Ross MacGibbon
Peter Manuira
Oliver Manzi
Clare Palmer
Celina Parker
Oriel Rodriguez
Panayiotis Sinnos
Helen Sprott
Nikki Weston
Margret Williams
Jan Younghusband

TECHNICAL
Guy Davies
Andy Downie
Jeremy Duncan
Andrew Ellis
James Fickling
Chantal Hauser
Billy Hiscoke
Mike Lindsay
John MacKenzie
Simon Reynolds
Tim Routledge
Russell Scott
Lucy Serjeant
Ben Stevens
Alistair Wilson

WARDROBE
Mal Barton
Ana Buckley
Kate Butterworth
Gabrielle Firth
Sonja Harms
James Kelly
Juan Leirado
Leila Ransley
Phil Reynolds
Jackie Risman
Bettine Roynon
Fiona Trippett
Sten Vollmuller

MAJOR FUNDERS
Anonymous
Audrey Sacher Charitable Trust
Bernard and Nadine Taylor
Charles Glanville
David Browne and Andrew Ellis
Derek Butler Trust
Esmee Fairbairn Foundation
Geoff Westmore
George and Angie Loudon
Ian Mactaggart Trust
Jack Petchey Foundation
John and Jane Trevitt
John Brooks
Marina Kleinwort
Michael Wakeford
Quercus Trust
R.M. Burton Charitable Trust
Robert Gavron Charitable Trust
Roby Swan
Serena Prest
Steve Springwood
The Baring Foundation
The Britten Estate Ltd
The Clore Duffield Foundation
The Denise Cohen Charitable Trust
The Foundation for Sport and the Arts
The Foyle Foundation
The Goldsmiths Company
The Helen Hamlyn Trust
The Linbury Trust
The Mercers Company
The Monument Trust
The Paul Hamlyn Foundation
The Philip and Psiche Hughes Trust
The Swan Trust

Ballet Boyz are Associate Artists of Sadler's Wells

THOSE WHO HAVE HELPED WITH THIS BOOK
Panayiotis Sinnos, Kerry Whelan and James McMenemy

PHOTOGRAPHER INDEX

SPECIAL THANKS
Bella and Beck, George, Rudi, Joseph, Zachary and Elijah